FORERUNNERS: IDEAS FIRST FROM THE UNIVERSITY OF
MINNESOTA PRESS

Original e-works to spark new scholarship

FORERUNNERS: IDEAS FIRST is a thought-in-process series of
breakthrough digital works. Written between fresh ideas and fin-
ished books, Forerunners draws on scholarly work initiated in nota-
ble blogs, social media, conference plenaries, journal articles, and
the synergy of academic exchange. This is gray literature publish-
ing: where intense thinking, change, and speculation take place in
scholarship.

T0149086

The End of Man

The End of Man
A Feminist Counterapocalypse

Joanna Zylinska

University of Minnesota Press

MINNEAPOLIS

Published by the University of Minnesota Press, 2018
111 Third Avenue South, Suite 290
Minneapolis, MN 55401-2520
http://www.upress.umn.edu

The University of Minnesota is an equal-opportunity educator and employer.

Contents

First as Tragedy . . .

THE END OF MAN: A FEMINIST COUNTERAPOCALYPSE offers an ironic take on one of the dominant apocalyptic narratives of our times. The prophecy contained in the book's title ostensibly points to the extinction of the human species, yet it also signals the expiration of the White Christian Man as the key subject of history. Embracing the spirit of the Forerunners: Ideas First series in its speculative mode and lighthearted style, this short book arises out of my recent interventions—conference papers, panel discussions, and artistic engagements—into the planetary crisis that embraces the environment, economy, and politics, as well as life itself. Specifically, *The End of Man* offers a challenge to the widespread belief that salvation from the current planetary apocalypse will come from a secularized yet godlike elsewhere: an escape to heavens in the form of planetary relocation, or an actual upgrade of humans to the status of gods via Artificial Intelligence (AI). Such solutions from elsewhere are currently being proposed by science and technology but they are also very much part of our political landscape. As well as looking suspiciously at various technocratic promises coming from Silicon Valley, *The End of Man* interrogates the current rise in populism worldwide, which is evident in the turning to the antiexpert solutions offered by self-proclaimed saviors from outside the political mainstream. In response, the book offers a vision of a "feminist counterapocalypse" that, in adopting precarity as the fundamental condition of living in the global postindustrial world, contests many of the masculinist and technicist solutions to said crisis.

Apocalypse, Now!

MORE BROADLY, *The End of Man* is designed as a critical intervention into what is currently being treated as a defining concept of our times: the Anthropocene. Posited as a new geological epoch in which human influence on the geo- and biosphere has been irreversible, the Anthropocene has become a new epistemological filter through which we humans can see ourselves. It has also triggered the production of multiple images and narratives about ourselves and about the world around us. The Anthropocene is often presented as a consequence of the excessive use of the resources of our planet, whereby seemingly interminable growth eventually leads to depletion, scarcity, and the crisis of life in its biological and social aspects. The term encapsulates not just "peak oil," "peak red meat," "peak growth," and "peak stuff," but also, perhaps more ominously, "peak man."[1] The Anthropocene is therefore a story about a presently unfolding planetary emergency that affects both rich and poor regions of the world—although not all of them with

---

1. Steve Howard, head of sustainability for IKEA, quoted in Zi-Ann Lum, "Steve Howard, Ikea Exec, Says The World Has Hit 'Peak Stuff,'" *Huffington Post,* January 20, 2016, http://www.huffingtonpost.ca/2016 /01/19/ikea-peak-home-furnishing-stuff_n_9019476.html.

the same impact or intensity. Yet it is worth pointing out that the apocalyptic tropes that underpin the Anthropocene narrative have actually been reoccurring through Western (and non-Western) cultural history—from premodern religious texts such as the Epic of Gilgamesh, the Book of Daniel, and the Book of Revelation (also known as the Apocalypse of Saint John) to contemporary cultural productions such as Federico Fellini's *La Dolce Vita*, Margaret Atwood's dystopian novels including *The Handmaid's Tale* and *MaddAddam*, and TV series such as *Survivors* and *The Walking Dead*. Critic Frank Kermode has pointed out that "apocalypse and the related themes are strikingly long-lived," while theologian Catherine Keller has gone so far as to suggest that "we stand . . . in an unfinished history of apocalyptic finalities."[2]

At the same time, the reoccurring apocalyptic narrative, in all its deadly guises, has acquired a new lease of life and a new sense of direction after becoming linked to the Anthropocene. Although the latter term has only gained currency in scientific and popular debates in the last few years, the beginning of the Anthropocene epoch is variously dated to the early days of agriculture, the launch of the Industrial Revolution in the eighteenth century, and the "great acceleration" of population growth and energy use in the years after 1945. Human and non-human extinction, and the destruction of life as we know it on our planet, loom as the end point of this epoch. Interestingly, the inflection of this particular apocalyptic narrative changes depending on who is telling the story. For example, the con-

2. Frank Kermode, *The Sense of an Ending: Studies in the Theory of Fiction* (Oxford: Oxford University Press, 2000), 29; Catherine Keller, *Apocalypse Now and Then: A Feminist Guide to the End of the World* (Boston: Beacon Press, 1996; Minneapolis: Fortress Press, 2005), 2. Citations refer to the Fortress Press edition.

cept of the Anthropocene can be used to establish an inherent link between capitalism and the modern way of life, and thus alert us to the injustices of the ever-encroaching neoliberal market logic that has now absorbed nature and climate under its remit.[3] But it can also be mobilized to praise human ingenuity and problem-solving skills, and to promote capital-driven solutions to climate change such as nuclear fission, carbon offsetting, and geoengineering.[4] Scientists still have not unequivocally agreed that the declaration of a new epoch is warranted, yet the Anthropocene has already been renamed by cultural and political theorists as the Anthrobscene, the Capitalocene, the Chthulucene, the Eurocene, the Plantationocene, and the Technocene, by way of challenging the inequality and injustice the original name was said to perpetuate. So even though we are nowhere near solving the Anthropocene's climate issues, in some areas of critical theory we already find ourselves post-Anthropocene, it seems.[5]

My own critical intervention involves delving into the knot of material processes, objects, and meanings that have accrued around this term in recent years in a variety of academic disciplines and in the wider cultural and media landscape. Rather than attempt to offer large-scale solutions to global ecological problems, or even to undertake a detailed critique of the various positions on the Anthropocene that have emerged from dif-

---

3. See Naomi Klein, *This Changes Everything: Capitalism vs. the Climate* (New York: Simon & Schuster, 2014).

4. See Mark Lynas, *The God Species: Saving the Planet in the Age of Humans* (Washington, D.C.: National Geographic, 2011), Kindle edition.

5. Claire Colebrook has gone so far as to argue: "We have *always* been post-Anthropocene." Claire Colebrook, "We Have Always Been Post-Anthropocene: The Anthropocene Counterfactual," in *Anthropocene Feminism*, ed. Richard Grusin (Minneapolis: University of Minnesota Press, 2017): 1–20.

ferent intellectual and political quarters, my aims in this book are more modest. I am predominantly interested in exploring the "structures of mourning" that the Anthropocene has both drawn upon and ushered in as its affective framework and intellectual foundation.[6] My focus is on the aforementioned "peak man," the impending population excess that will put unbearable constraints on our planet and that is consequently being posited by some as a harbinger of the end of the human species. Tracing the apocalyptic undertones of the Anthropocene story as a story of the existential crisis of humanity, I want to look at a number of recent developments surrounding the human both as a philosophical concept and as meaty materiality: the panic about the scarcity of resources available to sustain us, concerns over the aging of populations, renewed activity around AI on the part of Silicon Valley researchers and investors, and biotechnology research into ways of upgrading the human all the way to immortality. Last but not least, I want to locate the recent turn to the Anthropocene as an explanatory concept against the horizon of various current political events across the globe: the war on terror, the rise of rightwing populism, the refugee crisis, the Trump phenomenon, Brexit.

With all these different conceptual threads and points of inquiry, what I am concerned about first and foremost are the unspoken anxieties, desires, and fantasies that the finalism denoted by the "end of man" prophecy linked with the Anthropocene implies. I want to pay particular attention to the gendering of the Anthropocene story, with a view to querying some of its foundational assumptions and underpinning structures. Through this, I aim to take some steps toward sketching

6. Tom Cohen and Claire Colebrook, preface to *Twilight of the Anthropocene Idols,* by Tom Cohen, Claire Colebrook, and J. Hillis Miller (London: Open Humanities Press, 2016), 11.

a different narrative for the human subject who, once again, finds *him*self on the precipice of time. I also wish to engender a more anchored, embodied, and localized sense of response to, and responsibility for, the milieu we earthlings call home. "The end of man" pronounced as part of the current apocalyptic discourse can therefore be seen as both a promise and an ethical opening rather than solely as an existential threat. If the Anthropocene names a period in which the human has become a geological agent, my plan is to cut through some of the sedimented layers of meaning that have already accrued around the Anthropocene; to carve a better, more responsive, and more responsible picture of ourselves, here and now.

Ultimately, the goal of the book is to break what Keller has termed "an apocalypse habit." This habit manifests itself in a "wider matrix of unconscious tendencies" that shape finalist thinking, with its moralistic underpinnings, whereby moralism comes at the expense of the analysis of power relations on the ground.[7] My method involves working through and across various academic and popular narratives on the Anthropocene. Temporally, *The End of Man* is a follow-up to my earlier book, *Minimal Ethics for the Anthropocene,* but it is also a parallel or even an alternative project.[8] While it shares the conceptual spectrum and minimalism of form of the previous volume, as well as a desire to make a critical intervention into debates about the world in all its geophysical formations, *The End of Man* also offers a different pathway through the Anthropocene debate. This path does not lead so much via philosophy and

7. Keller, *Apocalypse Now and Then,* 10–11.

8. Joanna Zylinska, *Minimal Ethics for the Anthropocene* (Ann Arbor, Mich.: Open Humanities Press, 2014), http://www.openhumanitiespress.org/books/titles/minimal-ethics-for-the-anthropocene/.

ethics but rather traces the adaptation and transformation of philosophical ideas in a broader set of cultural scripts: journalism and wider media debates, sci-tech industry narratives, explicit and implicit religious beliefs, and political events.

Man's Tragic Worldview

APOCALYPTIC THINKING is an aspect of what has been termed "the tragic worldview": a cognitive framework that stands for the human's ability to reflect on life's finitude, coupled with the human's inability to *come to terms* with this finitude. This tension between cognitive states evokes a sense of tragedy in the human, with apocalypse becoming a symptom of thinking in tragic terms. Citing historian of religion Mircea Eliade, Polish philosopher Wojciech Załuski claims that the tragic worldview, which is still with us, superseded the prehistorical mental schema linked with the early cosmic religions. In that originary schema, the human experienced him- or herself as an undifferentiated part of nature and sensed death as just a temporary and insignificant disturbance within the ongoing permanence of life. Then, through the historical process of individuation, the human gradually became separated from the natural world while also learning to grasp the discontinuity of life—both human and nonhuman. For Załuski, a conservative Catholic thinker, the tragic worldview thus presents itself as a logical consequence of the human's separation from nature. The tragedy arises out of the impossibility of reconciling the appreciation of life in an amoral sense—that is, the ability to experience wonder and admire beauty as such—with the inability to hold on to those sensations and the objects from which they arise. The sense of the world's evanescence is thus a cornerstone of the tragic worldview.[1]

The tragic worldview arguably manifests itself in the fatalism of Homer and other ancient Greek thinkers, but it also returns, in modern guise, in the Dionysianism of Friedrich Nietzsche and the existentialism of Jean-Paul Sartre and Albert Camus. Significantly, the pretragic worldview associated with early naturalistic religions and with alternative cosmologies that Western thought subsequently deemed "primitive" has never been entirely superseded: it has become manifest in philosophies as diverse as Epicurean hedonism, Stoicism, and Buddhism. Yet Załuski, in his attachment to his own religious framework, sees the transition from the cosmic to the tragic worldview as a sign of the maturation of the human mind and thus as a teleological process of growth and progression beyond the state of nature. The philosophy of immanence developed by Gilles Deleuze, for example, would therefore be seen as immature from a particularist Christian viewpoint. Indeed, for Załuski, the process of human maturation as a species entails the gradual discovery of an authentic human condition: the condition of the fall from grace, or separation from God as the fullness of being. The human's very existence in and care about the world can only be apprehended in the course of history. The inherent tragedy of human existence resulting from its finitude is ultimately redeemed in Christianity by the promise of eternal life.

It is worth analyzing these conservative finalist discourses, especially in their Biblical articulations, because many of their

1. See Wojciech Załuski, *Przeciw rozpaczy: O tragicznej wizji świata i sposobach jej przezwyciężania* (Krakow: Copernicus Center Press, 2014).

tropes and figures return in the dominant narratives on the Anthropocene—the latter's apparent secularism premised on scientific rationality notwithstanding. And thus, when the sixth seal of the divine scroll is broken in the Book of Revelation, it unveils the wrath of God by proclaiming the total destruction of the stable planetary configuration, with all humans, irrespective of their wealth and status, rushing to hide from the catastrophe amid the ensuing rubble:

> There was a great earthquake; and the sun became black as sack-cloth of hair, and the moon became as blood;
> And the stars of heaven fell unto the earth. . . .
> And the heaven departed as a scroll when it is rolled together; and every mountain and island were moved out of their places.
> And the kings of the earth, and the great men, and the rich men, and the chief captains, and the mighty men, and every bondman, and every free man, hid themselves in the dens and in the rocks of the mountains.[2]

The sense of total annihilation is nevertheless overcome in the Book of Revelation by the promise of the New Heaven and Earth, or the New Jerusalem, with the river of life revitalizing the people and the tree of life offering them unlimited abundance.[3]

This kind of Biblical apocalyptic imaginary has provided modern humans with a framing device for understanding many of the current issues surrounding the Anthropocene: we can think here of images of the blackening of the sun as a result of fossil fuel use, pictures of land erosion and collapse (of "heaven falling unto the earth") due to mining, or reports of lands such as the Solomon Islands and the Maldives being "moved out of their places" due to rising ocean levels. Yet, more worryingly, it

2. Rev. 6:12–15 (King James Version).
3. See Rev. 21–22 (KJV).

is not just for diagnostic purposes that redemptive apocalyptic tropes are being mobilized today; they are also resorted to when solutions are offered. Indeed, there is a very clear sense in many of the science papers on the Anthropocene and their popularized media versions that the salvation from the Anthropocene's alleged finalism will come from a secularized yet godlike elsewhere: an escape to heavens (i.e., a planetary relocation) or an actual upgrade of humans to the status of *Homo deus*. In both of these narratives Man arrives in the post-Anthropocene New Jerusalem fully redeemed—and redesigned.

This supposedly individuated Man remains undifferentiated, both sexually and biologically. Indeed, the Man of the tragic worldview achieves his status at the cost of sacrificing sexual and biological difference that is always more than one. Disavowing his kinship with women and those of nonbinary gender, with animals, microbes, and fungi, Man separates from "nature" to emerge standing, proudly erect, yet already threatened with contamination, shrinkage, and evanescence. This disavowal is a condition of the preservation of Man's self-belief and self-appointed authority, allowing him continued "dominion over the fish of the sea, and over the fowl of the air, and over the cattle, and over all the earth, and over every creeping thing that creepeth upon the earth."[4]

4. Gen. 1:26 (KJV).

Men Repair the World for Me

IN A 2008 ESSAY TITLED "Men Explain Things to Me," Rebecca Solnit, an accomplished writer, recounts her encounter at a party in Aspen with "an imposing man who'd made a lot of money."[1] Having just published a book on time, space, and technology in the work of photographer Eadweard Muybridge, Solnit responded to the man's query about her writing career with an attempt to describe her latest project, only to be interrupted and told that another "very important book" on the subject had come out recently, and that he had read about it in the *New York Times Book Review*. Her friend's multiple interjections that it was actually Solnit's book the man was talking about were consistently ignored—until he eventually took it in, "went ashen," and then "began holding forth again." "Men explain things to me, and other women, whether or not they know what they're talking about," concludes Solnit. "Some men."[2] The essay struck a nerve with many readers and with women readers in particular because it captured, knowingly and poignantly, the ongoing gendering of dominant epistemologies.

1. Rebecca Solnit, "Men Explain Things to Me," *TomDispatch*, April 13, 2008, http://www.tomdispatch.com/post/174918.
2. Solnit, "Men Explain."

While I am wary of scoring points too easily by essentializing the political argument by pinning it to its author's gender identity—indeed, I would much rather quote Barack Obama than Sarah Palin on healthcare, Alain Juppé than Marine Le Pen on immigration, and Jeremy Corbyn than Theresa May on austerity—Solnit's intimations seem regrettably pertinent when it comes to the shaping of the Anthropocene narrative and the way it has been transmitted in both scholarly and mainstream literature. This is why I have decided to adapt her tongue-in-cheek phrase as a frame for approaching the Anthropocene story here. Interestingly, its central protagonist, Anthropocene Man, arrives on stage already lacking. Tom Cohen and Claire Colebrook ponder whether this Man isn't perhaps just "an effect of its own delusions of self-erasure."[3] They then go on to suggest, "Humanity comes into being, late in the day, when it declares itself to no longer exist, and when it looks wistfully, in an all too human way, at a world without humans. The human is an effect of a declaration of non-being: 'I do not exist; therefore I am.'"[4] The story about the end of man has actually been used thus to aggrandize Man as both subject and species, covering the foundational emptiness at its center as well as obscuring the very gesture of Man's erection *as man*. Kathryn Yusoff argues that "the Anthropocene has made man an end and origin in himself," in the process excluding or even impeding "the apprehension of important forms of differentiation and genealogical critique that might be useful in forestalling the continuation of the very conditions that produced this threshold moment."[5] It is thus not so much the actual gender of

3. Cohen and Colebrook, preface to *Twilight,* 11.
4. Cohen and Colebrook, preface to *Twilight,* 12.
5. Kathryn Yusoff, "Anthropogenesis: Origins and Endings in the Anthropocene," *Theory, Culture & Society* 33, no. 2 (2016): 3–28, 10–11.

the storytellers that troubles me about the Anthropocene narrative but rather the gendered mode and tenor of this narrative, with its messianic-apocalyptic undertones and its masculinist-solutionist ambitions.

As a result, the apocalyptic narrative of the Anthropocene also has an ontological dimension: it brings forth a temporarily wounded yet ultimately redeemed Man who can conquer time and space by rising above the geological mess he has created. The gender undertones of this new kind of planetary messianism reverberate through various articulations of the new epoch. When the Anthropocene Group, a subset of the International Commission on Stratigraphy, first convened in Berlin in 2014 to discuss whether the intensification of human activity deserved to be identified with a new term, "of the 29 scientists the working group listed on its website as members at the time of the meeting, only one was a woman."[6] This state of events prompted the *Guardian* journalist Kate Raworth to suggest: "Just call it the Manthropocene."[7] Again, it is not so much the number of men informing "us" about the Anthropocene—a situation that reflects first of all the structural gender "bias" of the sciences as such—that is of primary concern to me but rather the gendering of the Anthropocene debate coupled with its key authors' blindness to their own discursive tropes and points of reference, not to mention the sources drawn on and the authors cited.

And thus men explain the Anthropocene to me: I am thinking here of not just the members of the Stratigraphy commit-

6. Kate Raworth, "Must the Anthropocene Be a Manthropocene?," *Guardian,* October 20, 2014, https://www.theguardian.com /commentisfree/2014/oct/20/anthropocene-working-group-science -gender-bias. Following the international uproar over this, the number of women on the Committee has now increased, albeit only slightly.

7. Raworth, "Manthropocene?"

tee, led by Jan Zalasiewicz, but also other scientists, science writers, culture managers, and humanities scholars. Stephen Emmott, head of Microsoft's computational science research and author of the book *Ten Billion,* has declared "an unprecedented planetary emergency";[8] Bernd M. Scherer, Director of the Haus der Kulturen der Welt in Berlin, which ran a two-year Anthropocene project, has announced, "We have reached *a Tipping Point*";[9] while postcolonial historian Dipesh Chakrabarty has claimed that "what scientists have said about climate change challenges not only the ideas about the human that usually sustain the discipline of history but also the analytic strategies that postcolonial and post-imperial historians have deployed in the last two decades in response to the postwar scenario of decolonization and globalization."[10] The latter is particularly telling because, in the disciplinary conjuncture that has been at the forefront of challenging the normative gendering and racialization of the human subject, the return to the human as the agent of history has ushered back in many previously contested concepts and units of analysis—science, objectivity, nature, environment, crisis—with the sexless yet so-very-gendered Man being elevated back to the center point of both investigation and action. And thus, as Colebrook highlights, "After years of theory that contested every naturalization of what was ultimately historical and political, 'man' has

8. Stephen Emmott, *Ten Billion* (Harmondsworth, UK: Penguin, 2013), Kindle edition.

9. Bernd M. Scherer, preface to *Grain Vapor Ray: Textures of the Anthropocene,* eds. Katrin Klingan et al., vol. 4, *Manual* (Cambridge, Mass.: MIT Press, 2015), 3; emphasis in original.

10. Dipesh Chakrabarty, "The Climate of History: Four Theses," *Eurozine,* October 30, 2009, http://www.eurozine.com/the-climate -of-history-four-theses/. First published in *Critical Inquiry* 35, no. 2 (Winter 2009): 197–222.

returned."[11] Chakrabarty and others seem to be telling us that there is no time for textualist language games and other humanities pastimes anymore because "scientists," *telling it like it is,* have issued us with a more urgent task: we have to save the world and ourselves in it. The Anthropocene narrative therefore carries with it an injunction issued to "humanity as such" to move forward quickly and urgently while there is still time. Significantly, Cohen and Colebrook point out that the narrative of humans as a destructive species has not only generated the imperative to survive—"If 'we' discover ourselves to be an agent of destruction, then 'we' must re-form, re-group and live on"[12]—it has also produced what they term a "hyper-humanism," which I would like to rename here as Project Man 2.0.

11. Claire Colebrook, "What Is the Anthropo-political?," in *Twilight of the Anthropocene Idols,* ed. Tom Cohen, Claire Colebrook, and J. Hillis Miller (London: Open Humanities Press, 2016), 89.

12. Cohen and Colebrook, preface to *Twilight,* 9.

Project Man 2.0

AS BACKGROUND TO THESE DEVELOPMENTS, the temporality of the Anthropocene has brought with it a return to more interconnected models of understanding the world that have much in common with premodern frameworks: the ecological thinking that arises out of Earth systems science, the related notion of the world as Gaia promoted by Bruno Latour and Isabel Stengers, the idea of species companionship proposed by Donna Haraway, or the entangled human–nonhuman ontologies of Karen Barad and Anna Lowenhaupt Tsing. Indeed, Tsing highlights that "interspecies entanglements that once seemed the stuff of fables are now materials for serious discussion among biologists and ecologists, who show how life requires the interplay of many kinds of beings."[1] In a seeming rebuke to the teleological and progressivist narrative of Man's cognitive ascent, she also points out that "women and men from around the world have clamored to be included in the status once given to Man. Our riotous presence undermines the moral intentionality of Man's Christian masculinity, which

1. Anna Lowenhaupt Tsing, *The Mushroom at the End of the World: On the Possibility of Life in Capitalist Ruins* (Princeton, N.J.: Princeton University Press, 2015), vii.

separated Man from Nature."[2] This new post-Enlightenment mode of thinking that demotes the White Christian Man from his position as the subject of reason and the telos of our planet entails a promise of decolonizing our established frameworks of thought. But, perhaps unsurprisingly, it also becomes a horizon against which actions aimed at returning to Man's singular ontology and elevated stature are currently being performed.

Unfolding against this entangled human–nonhuman horizon, Project Man 2.0 entails a secular mobilization of the religious imaginary with singular Man now rebranded as *Homo deus*, or the God Species. The latter term has been used by journalist Mark Lynas in his popular science book of the same title, which outlines what I earlier described as a "solutionist" approach to climate change. Lynas's volume belongs to the genre of conversion narratives. A lapsed environmentalist who spent years destroying genetically modified crops in order to protect "nature," Lynas eventually saw the light. He describes how he gradually realized not only that the green movement was not a solution to planetary problems but also that it often exacerbated those problems—by facilitating the construction of coal plants in places where nuclear plants had been canceled, for example.[3] For the newly enlightened Lynas, any solutions to the planet's problems have to lie in conscious planetary management on the part of humans, who must embrace science-backed solutions while giving up on any fantasies of uncontaminated nature. So far, so blandly unproblematic.

Yet, *The God Species* has a weird parochialism to it. This manifests in the proposal to abandon any such unpleasantries

2. Tsing, *Mushroom*, vii.

3. Will Storr, "Mark Lynas: Truth, Treachery and GM Food," *Observer*, March 9, 2013, https://www.theguardian.com/environment/2013/mar/09/mark-lynas-truth-treachery-gm.

as calls for limiting human economic growth and productivity or, God forbid, "capitalism, the profit principle, or the market."[4] Lynas suggests we focus instead on identifying "a safe space in the planetary system within which humans can operate and flourish indefinitely in whatever way they choose."[5] The tone for this argument is already set in the book's hubristic opening: an account of entrepreneur J. Craig Venter's experiment with synthesizing life, retold as a neo-Biblical story. The book starts: "Then Man said: 'Let there be life.' And there was life."[6] What is meant by the latter is that the synthetic genome Venter had developed in his lab in 2010 started reproducing—except this is not the full story. Venter's team had to insert the computer-manufactured genome into an already existing nonsynthetic wet bacterial cell, from which the genome's native DNA had been extracted, thus merely enacting some lifelike processes in a medium that already supported what biology conventionally recognizes as life instead of creating any such life from scratch. This small ontological distinction notwithstanding, Lynas positions Venter as a kind of mischievous hacker of not just life as we know it but also of the Book of Genesis, with "God's power . . . now increasingly being exercised by us."[7] This is the story of creation as rewritten by venture capitalists, asserting "unchallenged dominion over all living things."[8] Yet Lynas seems oblivious to the political consequences of this shift. Indeed, his description of it by means of theological metaphors obscures the unequal distribution of the consequences of human-induced planetary intervention

4. Lynas, *The God Species.*
5. Lynas, *The God Species.*
6. Lynas, *The God Species.*
7. Lynas, *The God Species.*
8. Lynas, *The God Species.*

and instead positions the Anthropocene in terms of a supposedly eternal struggle of Man vs. Nature.

Our recently acquired godlike status still needs some tweaking, though. Lynas admits that all is not yet quite well in the Anthropocene paradise. "As if God were blind, deaf, and dumb, we blunder on without any apparent understanding of either our power or our potential."[9] But it is just a matter of time, and more important, technological innovation and economic investment, before things get sorted out. We thus need not worry: our "rebel nature" is a guarantee of success. In fact, Lynas admits to being tired of "the idea of perennial human victimhood" and thus offers to reboot the human as a god species whose only trajectory is upward—as long as we do not get bogged down by the melancholy narratives of the antiprogress brigade.[10] His is therefore a version of what Erle Ellis, another ecoentrepreneur, has called a "good Anthropocene": one in which humans can be proud of their achievements rather than lose too much sleep over their side effects. This approach is premised on "loving and embracing our human nature."[11] But the "Good Anthropocene" is really a new version of the Good Man, a prelapsarian Adam that can go back to and commune with God while also knowing that God is nothing else but a mirror image of his own self.[12] At the end of the day there is *just Adam*: a white Christian Adam,

9. Lynas, *The God Species*.

10. Lynas, *The God Species*.

11. Erle Ellis, "Stop Trying to Save the Planet," *Wired*, May 6, 2009, https://www.wired.com/2009/05/ftf-ellis-1/.

12. For an account of the idea of "the good Anthropocene," see "The Breakthrough Dialogue," The Breakthrough Institute, http://thebreakthrough.org/index.php/dialogue/past-dialogues/breakthrough-dialogue-2015. See also, for a critique of this concept, Rory Rowan, "Extinction as Usual? Geo-social Futures and Left Optimism," *e-flux journal* 65, SUPERCOMMUNITY, (May–August 2015): 1–11.

playing with himself. There's no God, no serpent—and, perhaps most significantly of all, no Eve. Indeed, no Eve gets a say in Lynas's New Jerusalem, as it has been designed as a safe space in which the White Man can safely rejoice in his own ingeniousness. There is also no dissensus, no conflict, and no inherent contradiction in the wishes and desires of the inhabitants of this safe space—because they are all just (imaginary) clones of our Man 2.0. It is perhaps understandable that Lynas should therefore joyfully declare: "This is no time for pessimism."[13] However, when listening to his story about planetary catastrophes and ways of overcoming them, we should be mindful of Keller's reflection that an apocalyptic narrative is "absolutely optimistic for its own believers, though radically pessimistic as to human historical aspirations."[14] In the world of Lynas and his postnature ecomates, it is Eve and other earthly creatures that have become extinct.

These historical aspirations on the part of the human may soon be superseded anyway because their holder will himself undergo a planetary transformation. The apocalyptic-sounding "end of man" will therefore be an upgrade instead: an evolution of the fleshy model that is becoming obsolete in the face of the current planetary challenges. And if the planet is proving to be more and more uninhabitable, the next logical step for the redeemers of today is to reach for what Lynas calls, without irony, a "techno-fix." This perhaps explains the renewed interest on the part of Silicon Valley visionaries in 1980s cyborg discourses, which are now returning in the guise of human-enhancement research, gerontology and, mutatis mutandis, AI. It is significant that the Anthropocene should usher in not just apocalyptic narratives

13. Lynas, *The God Species.*
14. Keller, *Apocalypse Now and Then,* 6.

about the disappearance of Man as a species but also redemptive discourses about the human's upgrade—that is, about the remodeling of the old design for the post–global warming era—coupled with research into longevity and "disrupting death." Man 2.0 as *Homo deus* seems to be a fulfillment of a prophecy issued by entrepreneur Stuart Brand of *Whole Earth Catalog* fame: "We are as gods and have to get good at it."[15]

The notion of *Homo deus* has recently made a literal appearance in an eponymous volume penned by another visionary of the whole world: Yuval Noah Harari.[16] After *Sapiens,* his commercially successful cosmic history of the human set in "deep time," Harari has now turned his attention to the currently popular genre of secular prophecy, which nevertheless remains steeped in religious overtones.[17] Given that famines, plagues, and wars have been (supposedly) conquered, or at least reined in as far as the prosperous regions of the world are concerned, with sugar now being "more dangerous than gunpowder," the only barrier left is fleshiness itself, he claims.[18] Yet just as climate change is seen by the proponents of the good Anthropocene as requiring a technical fix, the anthropos himself is seen as fully fixable, to the extent that death becomes rebranded as a "technical glitch."[19] Citing research and investments into "solving death" by inventor Ray Kurzweil, Google Ventures investment-fund manager Bill Marris, and PayPal cofounder Peter Thiel,

---

15. Lynas, *The God Species.*

16. I am using the phrase "*Homo deus*" as per the accepted Latin capitalization of species names (e.g., Homo sapiens), unless I am referring to Yuval Noah Harari's book *Homo Deus* (London: Harvill Secker, 2016).

17. Yuval Noah Harari, *Sapiens: A Brief History of Humankind* (London: Harvill Secker, 2011).

18. Harari, *Homo Deus,* 16.

19. Harari, *Homo Deus,* 22.

Harari concludes: "The writing is on the wall: equality is out—immortality is in."[20] The fantasy of immaculate conception will thus be realized—seemingly by 2200, with others offering 2050 as the deadline—by installing Silicon Valley venture capitalists as fathers of immortality, (re)generating life one cell at a time.

Harari seems neutrally diagnostic most of the time, although occasionally his impassive narrative borders on the ironic or the critical—for example, when looking at the ideology of Dataism, which rebrands humans as data-processing units and then sets off to reap the benefits of this rebranding. Yet *Homo Deus* actually preserves a rather conservative version of Man as a future-proofed survivor with his organs regenerated and tissue replenished for generations to come—or replaced by more durable nonorganic parts. Such developments occur against the Uncanny Valley of Silicon Capital, with its geoeconomic fault lines obscured by the Nasdaq indices. Even though Harari mischievously recognizes that any effort to predict what the world will look like in a hundred or two hundred years is "a waste of time," as "any worthwhile prediction must take into account the ability to re-engineer human minds, and this is impossible," his present account of the developmental direction is still focused on the human as a stand-alone, discrete entity.[21] Harari's chapter on the Anthropocene thus ends with an unacknowledged humanist triumphalism, whereby the ostensible critique of the humanist model, propped up by notions such as the soul, language, or individuality, ends up celebrating human ingenuity. This is the ingenuity of the human subject who will eventually upgrade himself into a god thanks to his evolved ability to cooperate with others, but also that of the male human author

20. Harari, *Homo Deus*, 25.
21. Harari, *Homo Deus*, 46.

narrating this story of the secular human's return to the biblical tree of knowledge via physics, chemistry, and biology. What is missing from Harari's account is an awareness and acknowledgment of the very gesture on the part of this human author to *carve out* the Homo sapiens as a discrete entity, to extricate *him* from *his* various material and political entanglements and dependencies, and to speculate about *his* developmental trajectory into the future, his radical evolution of the mind, his "merging with robots and computers."[22] Harari does recognize that the human is just another kind of animal, and he actually makes numerous pitches for veganism as the only ethically defensible stance with regard to coexisting with other species. Yet the epistemological orientation of his time travel remains firmly in place: Harari's arrow of time still flies alongside the history of Man as we know him, only slightly more reengineered. The problem, therefore, lies not with the cognitive restrictions that the future imposes on us. Rather, it lies with the cognitive blind spot Harari himself brings to his own understanding of the human as a discrete subject of history: a diminished yet ultimately solipsistic Robocop who may just succeed in getting away with the whole Anthropocene unpleasantness because he is better than other species at teaming up with other Robocops and at inventing and transmitting stories to his genetic kin. (Rats, cockroaches, and microbes, no obvious storytellers as far as we can tell, will most likely prove him wrong.)

22. Harari, *Homo Deus,* 49.

Exit Man

SHOULD MAN'S UPGRADE PROCESS FAIL or take too long, however, an alternative counter-Anthropocene plan is currently under development: Man's planetary relocation. Faced with the prospect of an impending apocalypse on Earth, many scientists, inventors, and entrepreneurs are already lining up to embark on a celestial trip. Wheelchair-bound theoretical physicist Stephen Hawking has joined the line, announcing recently:

> We need a new generation of explorers to venture out into our solar system and beyond. These first private astronauts will be pioneers, and I hope to be among them. . . . I believe in the possibility of commercial space travel—for exploration and for the preservation of humanity. I believe that life on Earth is at an ever-increasing risk of being wiped out by a disaster, such as a sudden nuclear war, a genetically engineered virus, or other dangers. I think the human race has no future if it doesn't go to space.[1]

The supposed inevitability of cross-planetary migration is usually presented via the familiar colonizing rhetoric, with its gendered assumptions about dominion and conquest and its eschatological

---

1. Stephen Hawking, "I Think the Human Race Has No Future If it Doesn't Go to Space," *Guardian*, September 26, 2016, https://www.theguardian.com/science/2016/sep/26/i-think-the-human-race-has-no-future-if-it-doesnt-go-to-space.

fantasies of the disembodied mind. It is actually unsurprising that Hawking should adopt this type of logic and argument because he perfectly epitomizes, through the ongoing mediated performance of his scholarly identity, the idea of Man as a singular self-sufficient genius. As argued by Hélène Mialet in her provocative and thought-provoking book *Hawking Incorporated: Stephen Hawking and the Anthropology of the Knowing Subject*, which analyzes the construction of the Hawking persona by the assemblage of human and nonhuman actors—"the computer/the synthesizer/the personal assistant/the graduate assistant/the nurses—that transforms a man deprived of speech and movement into 'the genius we all know,'" Hawking "has become an emblem for the ideology that dominates our understanding of science, namely, that science is practiced by disinterested scientists who are able to transcend the political, social, and cultural spaces that their bodies inhabit in order to live in the unadulterated world of the pure mind."[2] It is precisely this pure mind that becomes the driver of the currently awaited civilizational jump: one that is to occur either mentally, as in the singularity theory of Ray Kurzweil, which predicts an explosion of artificial superintelligence that will merge with or even take over the human mind; or literally, in the form of relocation to other planets. What is most interesting about Mialet's book is that she treats "Hawking" not as unique due to having to rely on an external network of collaborators and instruments because of his disability but rather as just an extreme-case scenario of many great men of science and history who have had to function as part of the intricate network of humans (wives, secretaries, cleaners, research assistants) and nonhumans (technologies of writing, computational machines, as well as lab, office, and

2. Hélène Mialet, *Hawking Incorporated: Stephen Hawking and the Anthropology of the Knowing Subject* (Chicago: University of Chicago Press, 2012), Kindle edition.

home infrastructures) in order to accomplish things. Yet these enmeshed networks have had to remain obscured for the myth of the singular genius to be developed and sustained.

I mention this issue here because the notion of the singular genius returns in current speculations on planetary travel, with attempts to take us there presented precisely as an adventure led by select bold, male pioneers bravely venturing where few would dare to go. The gendered connotations of these ambitions are quite explicit. Indeed, many hopeful space colonizers simply cannot wait to meet their "new Jerusalem, coming down from God out of heaven, prepared as a bride adorned for her husband."[3] Elon Musk, inventor and founder of Tesla Motors and SpaceX—the latter a company whose goal is to enable affordable space travel and the eventual colonization of Mars—is a case in point. Musk's "spiraling ambitions" are widely praised by Silicon Valley, "with commentators frequently comparing him to eponymous Iron Man superhero Tony Stark."[4] In the keynote presented in September 2016 at the 67th International Astronautical Congress in Guadalajara, Mexico, Musk explained that humanity faces "two fundamental paths" today: staying on Earth and eventually becoming extinct or developing into "a spacefaring civilization, and a multi-planetary species."[5]

Dreams of life on Mars have a long history, from the late nineteenth- to early twentieth-century writings of astronomer and

3. Rev. 21 (KJV).

4. Olivia Solon, "Elon Musk Has Ambitious Plans for Mars. Are They As Crazy As They Sound?," *Guardian*, September 27, 2016, https://www.theguardian.com/technology/2016/sep/27/elon-musk-spacex-mars-exploration-space-science.

5. Nicky Woolf, "SpaceX Founder Elon Musk Plans to Get Humans to Mars in Six Years," *Guardian*, September 28, 2016, https://www.theguardian.com/technology/2016/sep/27/elon-musk-spacex-mars-colony.

businessman Percival Lowell, who (erroneously) postulated the existence of canals, and thus of advanced alien life, on the Red Planet, through to the NASA Astrobiology Institute's "search for evidence of prebiotic chemistry and life on Mars and other bodies in our Solar System."[6] What is new about Musk's plan is not so much his desire to *find* life, sophisticated or emerging, on Mars but rather his ambition to *take life to Mars* in the form of human cargo. Indeed, Musk aims to establish a sustainable colony of one million people within the next forty to one hundred years—although he emphasizes that the first travelers must be "prepared to die." Planning to start colonization in 2022, he presented "a very aggressive schedule" to the large crowd gathered at the congress in Guadalajara, which went "absolutely wild" on hearing about his plans.[7] The main obstacle at the moment is the high cost of spacecraft construction, something Musk promises to address by developing a so-called "SpaceX Interplanetary Transport System." Musk's keynote was richly illustrated with seductive images of pointy and hard bullet-like rockets with rounded heads, steaming, throbbing, and then rising up to pierce the Earth's pink and soft atmosphere on their journey to Mars. It was CGI space porn of the highest caliber, and it was being lapped up by the wild crowd.[8]

6. Percival Lowell, *Mars* (Boston: Houghton, Mifflin, 1895); *Mars and Its Canals* (New York: The Macmillan Company, 1906); *Mars as the Abode of Life* (New York: The Macmillan Company, 1908); NASA website, quoted in Sarah Kember, ed., introduction to *Astrobiology and The Search for Life on Mars*, Living Books about Life (Ann Arbor, Mich.: Open Humanities Press, 2011), http://www.livingbooksaboutlife.org/books/Astrobiology.

7. Woolf, "SpaceX Founder."

8. Dave Mosher, Ali Sundermier and Rafi Letzter, "This Is Elon Musk's Plan to Begin Colonizing Mars by 2022," *Business Insider UK*, September 27, 2016, http://www.businessinsider.com/elon-musk-spacex -mars-colony-talk-iac-2016–9.

The End of the White Man

THE TWO FORMS OF TECHNOLOGICAL ESCAPISM *from* the Anthropocene described above—toward either the cyborgian future of Man 2.0 or the interplanetary future of World 2.0—have a more inward-looking counterpart, one that I call here, with a nod to science-fiction writer Stanisław Lem, "encystment." Lem uses this term in his philosophical treatise *Summa Technologiae* to describe the behavior of a civilization that is experiencing an information crisis and is thus threatened with the loss of control over its own homeostasis, a result of receiving too much feedback from what Lem calls "Nature." In response, such a civilization may become "encysted": it will construct "'a world within a world,' an autonomous reality that is not directly connected with the material reality of Nature."[1] Enveloping itself with a "cybernetic–sociotechnical shell," the encysted civilization becomes a world to itself, deferring, at least temporarily, the spectrum of information explosion, entropy, and its eventual demise.

The mechanism of encystment is regularly mobilized by various sections of the human population in an attempt to

1. Stanisław Lem, *Summa Technologiae,* trans. Joanna Zylinska (Minneapolis: University of Minnesota Press, 2013), 87.

ward off all kinds of threats, including the existential threat to our very existence as a species and to the continued survival of our terrestrial abode. The "cybernetic-sociotechnical shell," emerging today in the form of walls, barriers, bans, and exits, is fueled precisely by discourses of excess, mainly the excess of human bodies and their organic and nonorganic products. Thus, the progressive politics of degrowth on the planetary scale in the face of the Anthropocene finds, perhaps too easily, its ugly twin in the localized discourses of *information and matter overload*: cyberterrorism, multiculturalism, immigration flood, the refugee crisis. The fuel for the maintenance of such multiple encysted worlds is provided today by the logic of the self-same: the image of the foundational anthropos of the Anthropocene, whose manhood is now threatened by the inpour of those who are not like him. Nicholas Mirzoeff has gone so far as to argue that the Anthropocene is a manifestation of white supremacist tendencies because the threat it heralds pertains to the withering of the imperialist white male as the supposedly timeless subject of geohistory.[2] The rise of the global "alt-right" movement—which the UK's *Observer* has called "a nouvelle vague of racism"—is an example of the recent resurgence of those tendencies. In an interview with the *Observer*'s Sanjiv Bhattacharya, members of the alt-right American Freedom Party have declared a fight against "the systematic browbeating of the white male" and the "looming extinction of the white race."[3]

2. Mirzoeff writes: "Given that the Anthropos in *Anthropocene* turns out to be our old friend the (imperialist) white male, my mantra has become: it's not the Anthropocene, it's the white supremacy scene." Nicholas Mirzoeff, "It's Not the Anthropocene, It's the White Supremacy Scene; or, The Geological Color Line," in *After Extinction,* ed. Richard Grusin (Minneapolis: University of Minnesota Press, 2018).
3. Sanjiv Bhattacharya, "'Call Me a Racist, but Don't Say I'm a

When Mirzoeff makes a link between the Anthropocene and the colonization of America, thus claiming that the new geological epoch under discussion began "with a massive colonial genocide," and then goes on to suggest that "the political failure to enact change in relation to the crisis of the Earth system" may have been motivated "precisely by systemic racism," he sees the Anthropocene as a fact and as evidence of both colonialism and racism.[4] But what if the situation were even more scandalous than that? What if, without denying the constitutive relationship between violence and the emergence of the modern world that has been posited by many scholars (not least among them Walter Benjamin, Michel Foucault, and Jacques Derrida), we go one step further and actually suggest that the very emergence of the Anthropocene *as a proposition and discourse* has acted as fodder for white supremacist tendencies by way of containing and perhaps temporarily warding off anxieties about the extinction of the White Man? It is therefore interesting that, when commenting on the views of his alt-right interlocutors, Bhattacharya would conclude: "Their point is that white people are melting away like the icecaps, and they have a primal drive to stop it."[5] The abovementioned "encystment" is the solution the alt-right offers; in response to the threat of too much racial mixing, they advocate "Balkanisation: separate territories for separate tribes."[6] This thinking is underpinned by Man's somewhat confusing relationship to "Nature," which has to be explicitly overcome

Buddhist': Meet America's Alt Right," *Observer,* October 9, 2016, https://www.theguardian.com/world/2016/oct/09/call-me-a-racist-but-dont-say-im-a-buddhist-meet-the-alt-right.

    4. Mirzoeff, "It's Not the Anthropocene."

    5. Bhattacharya, "'Call Me a Racist.'"

    6. Bhattacharya, "'Call Me a Racist.'"

as the state of bestiality and wildness above which (the White) Man can rise yet remain implied as a justification for this hierarchy between races and "tribes."

As discussed earlier, the idea that the separation of Man from Nature signifies teleological maturation underpins the tragic vision of the world. This vision is ultimately redeemed in Christianity with the promise of salvation and eternal life. Yet apocalypticism has some serious consequences for the emergence of ethico-political frameworks on our planet. Keller argues that "endist individualism reinforces the secular myopias of U.S. [and not just U.S.—JZ] culture today—infantile cravings for gratification and rescue." She goes on to suggest that the successful politicization of right-wing Christians "allows the right to secretly harness the revolutionary horsepower of apocalypse," redirecting the force of the liberation encoded in the apocalyptic narrative, manifesting itself in revolutionary movements all over the world, into a backlash against those movements.[7] The apocalyptic discourse ultimately serves to maintain the status quo of the self-same White (Christian) Man and to protect him against what seems alien and hostile: women, transsexuals, refugees, the homeless. As Colebrook points out:

> The supposedly universal "human" was always white, Western, modern, able-bodied and heterosexual man; the "subject" who is nothing other than a capacity for self-differentiation and self-constitution is the self of market capitalism. To return to "anthropos," now, after all these years of difference seems to erase all the work in postcolonialism that had declared enlightenment "man," to be a fiction that allowed all the world to be "white like me," and all the work in feminism that exposed the man and subject of reason as he who cannibalizes all others and remakes them in his image. The Anthropocene seems

7. Keller, *Apocalypse Now and Then*, 56.

to override vast amounts of critical work in queer theory, trans-animalities, post-humanism and disability theory that had destroyed the false essentialism of the human.[8]

Anthropocene apocalypticism thus reveals itself to be nothing more than an exercise in narcissism: a denial of the "feeling of being the animal you are, born of other animals, made of mirroring them."[9] The denial of our animality takes place at the expense of projecting this animality onto others: the parasites of the accepted social and economic order, who become enclosed in detention centers and refugee camps such as the Calais "Jungle" camp in France, liquidated in October 2016. This mode of thinking and acting promotes species chauvinism with the elevation of Man over his animal companions and nonhuman constituents. It also leads to a return to nationalist or regionalist governance via encystment: a conservative politics of maintenance and preservation.

Importantly—and worryingly—the successful politicization of right-wing Christians in the light of the apocalyptic narratives identified by Keller has its wider aftermath in the resurgence of right-wing populism across the world as a (perhaps unwitting) response to the impending planetary cataclysm. Francisco Panizza offers a symptomatic reading of populism "as an anti-status quo discourse that simplifies the political space by symbolically dividing society between 'the people' (as the 'underdogs') and its '*other*.'"[10] The Anthropocene imagery provides a justification for the finalist pronouncements of many of the "postpolitical" politicians and their followers, with the *pop-*

8. Colebrook, "What Is the Anthropo-political?," 91.

9. Kristin Dombek, *The Selfishness of Others: An Essay on the Fear of Narcissism* (New York: Farrar, Straus & Giroux, 2016), Kindle edition.

10. Francisco Panizza, introduction to *Populism and the Mirror of Democracy*, ed. Francisco Panizza (London: Verso, 2005), 1–31, 3.

ulus elevated to the multiplicity of Man, seemingly threatened yet still standing tall. Arguably, we have been experiencing the rise of populism in the world, or even its arrival in recurring waves, for a while now. Panizza's edited collection *Populism and the Mirror of Democracy* came out in 2005 and already analyzed the growth of the right-wing populist FPÖ (Freedom Party of Austria) under Jörg Haider post-1986, the rise of the New Right in English Canada since 1987, the emergence of populist elements in the "new politics" of Carlos Menem in Argentina post-1989, the turn to populism in postapartheid South Africa in the 1990s, the emergence of skinhead conservatism out of Thatcherism in the UK between 1997 and 2001, and the success of the Pim Fortuyn electoral list in the Netherlands in 2002 following the consolidation of anti-immigration sentiments in the light of Fortuyn's political activities and subsequent murder. Yet 2016, the year that gave impetus to my book, saw an intensification of populist tendencies, evident in multiple world events from the Donald Trump phenomenon to Brexit. Of course, populist voices emerge in different parts of the world and do not exclusively appear on the (Christian) right, as evidenced in the deadly yet popular war on drugs and the racist, inflammatory anti–United States rhetoric of Rodrigo Duterte, the president of the Philippines.[11] They can also be heard in the "enlightened populism" of Emmanuel Macron or in the resurgence of left-wing populism as a political response to the changing affective composition of the electorate worldwide.[12] I

11. Ernesto Laclau has extensively analyzed populist tendencies in Latin America, focusing on various forms of left populism. See also John B. Judis, "Us v Them: The Birth of Populism," *Guardian,* October 13, 2016, https://www.theguardian.com/politics/2016/oct/13/birth-of -populism-donald-trump.

12. This phrase has been proposed by the Polish political commentator Sławomir Sierakowski. He is referring to a countertendency to the

am, however, particularly interested in the mobilization of populism as a weapon against perceived threats to the identity of the white Christian man, a figure embraced by many populist leaders as the quintessential mark of European civilization.

The political rhetoric mixing select tenets of the Christian faith and biblical fundamentalism has indeed played a role in the emergence of right-wing parties and positions in various parts of the globe in the early twenty-first century. Take, for example, Poland under the rule of the Law and Justice Party (PiS), with its consolidation of governmental power over various public institutions as well as citizens' private bodies and lives in 2016 following its electoral success the year before. Such rhetoric also arguably fueled the popularity of Donald Trump as presidential candidate that culminated in his election as president in November 2016—although Trump himself is no poster boy for religion. Yet religion is not a prerequisite for the emergence of conservative and conservationist populist sentiment: secular passion can easily take its place. At the risk of painting in rather thick brushstrokes, we can think here about diverse events such as the rejection of the European Union's migrant plan in the name of national sovereignty by Viktor Orbán's Hungary, Alternative für Deutschland's combat against the supposed threat of Islamification, post-Heider FPÖ's defense of "freedom and democracy" against the European Union with all its supposed diktats, or the mobilization of anti-European sentiment cultivated over the years via the power nexus of mainstream

---

right-wing populism promoted by politicians such as Poland's ex–prime minister Donald Tusk and France's Macron, who suspended any traditional affiliations with either left or right politics while offering a bland yet seductive mixture of optimism, progress, modernity, and prosperity in lieu of any coherent political program. In "Populizm oświecony," *Polityka* no. 20 (3110), May 17–23, 2017: 47–49.

media and politics in the UK that resulted in the 2016 referendum victory for Brexit supporters. Setting itself against the elitism and corruption of traditional politics, this recent form of populism still very much borrows from the Christian myth of redemption: it "offers a promise of emancipation after a journey of sacrifice."[13]

No matter whether the fuel for these political movements is religious or secular, its recent nemesis also tends to be a religious figure: the Muslim man. In populist political rhetoric, he is not always a terrorist but he is always potentially dangerous: he can become "radicalized," oppress his wife, assault "our" women, or end up a rapist. This explains the (il)logic behind Anders Behring Breivik's acts of mass murder in August 2012, first in Oslo and then on the summer-camp island of Utøya, of over seventy of his Norwegian compatriots whom he associated with "cultural Marxism." Not particularly religious himself, Breivik had a strong sense that European identity was formatively entangled with Christianity and that its key enemy was Islam. In his book *Heroes: Mass Murder and Suicide,* Italian philosopher Franco "Bifo" Berardi rather chillingly observes that "the fundamental political agenda of Mr Breivik is not so far removed from the agenda of conservative political movements the world over."[14] What we are witnessing in the pronouncements of their supporters, now increasingly visible thanks to the Internet and social media, is a defense of a particular version of Eurocentric identity which seems threatened with both Islamification and demasculinization. This is illustrated in the misogynist slide from "Muslim" to "woman" in Breivik's own rant: "Femininity is penetrating everywhere, and the feminiza-

13. Panizza, introduction to *Populism*, 23.
14. Franco Berardi, *Heroes: Mass Murder and Suicide* (London: Verso, 2015), 100. See also pages 96 and 110.

tion of European culture is nearly completed. Europe is a woman who would prefer to be raped than to risk serious injuries while resisting."[15]

Writing in the *New York Review of Books,* Jan-Werner Müller analyzes this "fundamental political conflict that can be found in many Western democracies today" precisely in terms of the fear of contamination and gender-otherness:

> This conflict is not meaningfully described as one of "ordinary people versus the establishment." In Austria, both the Freedom Party and the Green Party have been "established" since the mid-1980s; in Britain, Boris Johnson, one of the main faces of the Brexit campaign, is about as establishment as one can get in the UK; and Donald Trump is hardly the authentic representative of Main Street. Rather, on one side of the new conflict are those who advocate more openness: toward minorities at home and toward engagement with the world on the outside. On the other side we find the Le Pens, Farages, and Trumps: close the nation-state off by shutting borders and thereby, or so they promise, take back control; but also, preserve the traditional hierarchies that have come under threat on the inside. "Make America Great Again" means above all: "Make sure white males rule again."[16]

The abovementioned developments work on the basis of issuing what Ernesto Laclau has called "the promise of fullness": an impossible fantasy that provides a shelter against oncoming threats both real and imaginary.[17] The populist promise today involves the prospect of a land of plenty from a time long gone. Yet the desired object must remain unnamed as the very

15. Quoted in Berardi, *Heroes,* 99.

16. Jan-Werner Müller, "Austria: The Lesson of the Far Right," *New York Review of Books,* July 25, 2016, http://www.nybooks.com/daily/2016/07/25/austria-freedom-party-populism-lesson-far-right/.

17. Ernesto Laclau, "Populism: What's in a Name?," in *Populism and the Mirror of Democracy,* ed. Francisco Panizza (London: Verso, 2005), 32–49, 35.

survival of not just of the populist leader but also the postpolitical democratic consensus that allows for the emergence of populism depends on the survival and prosperity of the current political and economic regime. Acknowledging that "the people" yearn for a world before globalization and before neoliberal capitalism would involve a confrontation with the fact that this seemingly naturalized state of events is subject to change and that it may *need* to change. This is why few politicians who want to be seen as "electable" are promising, let alone successfully delivering, the reduction of the income gap, more accessible housing policies, or better access to healthcare.[18] Any of these would require a serious rethinking of the neoliberal economic model that the globalized world now depends on, and that is both a product of and a motor for the Anthropocene.[19] (As explained before, while attempts to date the Anthropocene go back variously to the early days of agriculture, the colonization of the New World, or the steam age, many thinkers point to the post-1945 intensification of manufacturing, extractivism, urbanization, and global transport and trade as its most significant markers.)[20] It is therefore far easier for the so-called "democratic center" to dismiss those harboring populist sympathies as xenophobes while adopting splinters of their demands:

18. The UK's Jeremy Corbyn, who, while still in the opposition in 2018, is transforming in public perception from an "unelectable" to a valid political opponent of the Conservative party, may prove an exception to this trend.

19. Trump's vague promises to put an end to globalization and "make America great again" are not coupled with any desire to eliminate economic inequality and are, indeed, aimed at strengthening the very same individualized political subject that underpins the neoliberal logic.

20. See, for example, J. R. McNeill and Peter Engelke, *The Great Acceleration: An Environmental History of the Anthropocene Since 1945* (Cambridge, Mass.: Harvard University Press, 2016).

anti-EU sentiment, support for "European values," immigration control. This development ends up leaving the political and economic status quo intact. Chantal Mouffe claims: "When democratic politics has lost its capacity to shape the discussion about how we should organise our common life, and when it is limited to securing the necessary conditions for the smooth working of the market, the conditions are ripe for talented demagogues to articulate popular frustration."[21] A response to this state of events leads to what Mouffe identifies as "moral condemnation and the establishment of a cordon sanitaire" around the populists, in place of engaging them in political struggle.[22] This is because there is no room for political struggle anymore in the era of economic consensus: there is only room for frustration, fury, persecution mania, and, more worryingly, depression and suicide.

21. Chantal Mouffe, "The 'End of Politics' and the Challenge of Right-Wing Populism," in *Populism and the Mirror of Democracy*, ed. Francisco Panizza (London: Verso, 2005), 55.
22. Mouffe, "'End of Politics,'" 57.

The End of Men?

"Suicide is the single biggest killer of men under 45 in the UK,"[1] and the second biggest cause of death of young males in the United States.[2] These statistics raise serious questions about the well-being of a large sector of populations in the so-called developed world. This state of events has found its literalization in a 2010 article in the *Atlantic* by Hannah Rosin titled "The End of Men," which was subsequently turned into a book.[3] A genre of "pop sociology meets apocalypticism to emerge triumphant in the end," Rosin's book does indeed discuss the gradual disappearance of men from various facets of

---

1. This statistic has been cited by Jane Powell, CEO of suicide prevention charity CALM (Campaign against Living Miserably), quoted in Sarah Hughes, "From Bruce Springsteen to Tyson Fury, Men Are Opening Up about Depression," *Guardian,* October 8, 2016, https://www.theguardian.com/society/2016/oct/08/men-depression-opening-up-kid-cudi-springsteen-fury.

2. "Leading Causes of Death in Males and Females, United States," Office of Minority Health & Health Equity, Centers for Disease Control and Prevention, http://www.cdc.gov/men/lcod/.

3. Hanna Rosin, "The End of Men," *Atlantic,* July/August 2010, http://www.theatlantic.com/magazine/archive/2010/07/the-end-of-men/308135/. See also Hanna Rosin, *The End of Men and the Rise of Women* (New York: Riverhead Books, 2012).

public and private life, yet it is ostensibly about the end of patriarchy. Her argument, backed with figures supposedly from all over the world (but with a strong bias toward Kansas), highlights the fact that there are more women today in every sector of education and the economy than there had been at any previous point in history, even if relatively few women occupy the topmost positions. What's more, the age-old preference for sons is also supposedly eroding worldwide. With industrial jobs disappearing and physical strength being removed from a typical list of essential workers' attributes, women are said to be thriving in the modern service economy. "What if modern, postindustrial society is simply better suited to women?" asks Rosin breezily.[4] Her analysis is not particularly scholarly or thorough: it is rooted in the deeply ideological assumption that "geopolitics and global culture are, ultimately, Darwinian."[5] Men are ending, claims Rosin, because they do not fit into the new economic model, with women's soft skills—"social intelligence, open communication, the ability to sit still and focus"[6]—better suited to the marketplace of what Franco "Bifo" Berardi has called semiocapitalism: "the contemporary regime of production in which capital valorization is based on the constant emanation of information flows."[7] The family structure has also changed, with women now setting the terms of the relationship and being less willing to devote their lives to playing a supporting role in a household—especially after they have lost respect for its prior male "head."

Even though a certain tone of lament over the prophesized "end of men" can be detected in Rosin's narrative, her story

4. Rosin, "End of Men."
5. Rosin, "End of Men."
6. Rosin, "End of Men."
7. Berardi, *Heroes*, 24.

ultimately lacks not only ethical compassion but also political understanding. Superficially empowering in the same way that Sheryl Sandberg's *Lean In* was said to be empowering, Rosin's argument is actually pernicious because it presents as natural the political decisions that have been taken with regard to the current dominant economic model and what counts as value within it, with derivatives, debts, and other forms of financial abstraction seen as more profitable than the material objects of labor and trade. In the process she demonstrates a limited understanding of both patriarchy—which for her seems to entail a competition between the sexes in which there can only be one winner—and of feminism, positioned as a process of catch-up with the system's inherent inequalities remaining firmly in place. It seems that in Rosin's universe gender relations can change to the extent that the domination of manhood can be sociobiologically weakened, but the economic system that sustains them cannot. In a rather scathing review of Rosin's book, Jennifer Homans has observed that "'The end of men' is the end of a manufacturing-based economy and the men who worked there, many of whom are now unemployed, depressed, increasingly dependent on the state and women to support them."[8] Yet, to paraphrase Fredric Jameson, it seems easier for Rosin to imagine the end of man than the end of capitalism.[9]

As should have become clear by now, my analysis in this book of the "end of man" is *not* meant to be yet another example of "men-bashing." On the contrary, my argument arises

8. Jennifer Homans, "A Woman's Place: 'The End of Men,' by Hanna Rosin," *New York Times*, September 13, 2012, http://www.nytimes.com/2012/09/16/books/review/the-end-of-men-by-hanna-rosin.html.

9. Fredric Jameson recalls a saying, "It is easier to imagine the end of the world than to imagine the end of capitalism," in "Future City," *New Left Review* 21, no. 1 (May–June 2003), http://newleftreview.org/II/21/fredric-jameson-future-city.

out of a deep concern for the lives of humans of different and diverse gender identifications, in all their nonhuman entanglements, under the finalist, apocalyptic conditions and narratives of the present day. So, even though the "end of man" may indeed signal the possible withering of a particular form of white Christian masculine subjectivity as the dominant orientation of our cultural and political discourses, it is meant to read as a diagnosis of a political condition and a positing of a political opportunity rather than as a psychological or biological diagnosis of the extinction of a particular species. (It also needs to be acknowledged that, structurally, there is nothing about the imaginary reign of, say, women that would guarantee a fullness of society and a happily ever after.) At the same time, this opportunity responds to the unfolding of a particular condition of economic and existential precarity explored by Bifo as a symptom of the current iteration of hypercapitalism, with the heroes of the age of production now turned into ghosts.[10] From this perspective, it makes sense to evoke finalism and the apocalypse because "surviving in such conditions means literally surviving the end of the world, in a condition of meaninglessness and loneliness, in a perpetual condition wherein the exchange of meaningful signs with one's fellow creatures is impossible."[11] It is in this context that the Trump phenomenon can be understood as not only the last gasp of a particular version of white masculinity but also as a symptom of a particular generational vulnerability.

Rather than bemoan the passing of macho heroism and thus symbolically reinstate it, Bifo issues a call for justice in the form of a requiem for the lives lost to suicide by young and

10. See Berardi, *Heroes*, 5.
11. Berardi, *Heroes*, 162.

middle-aged males in the global world, from the United States to Finland, Japan, India, and the Middle East. He argues that in the first two decades of the twenty-first century, a century "inaugurated by a monumental act of suicide" (i.e., 9/11), "suicide has come to be perceived increasingly as the only effective action of the oppressed, the only action which can actually dispel anxiety, depression and impotence."[12] By saying this, Berardi is not imposing any kind of moral relativism or equating terrorist suicide attacks with individual suicides of distressed postlaborers. What he *is* doing is recognizing various manifestations of a self-destructive tendency at the core of contemporary masculinity, which he links with multiple sociopolitical developments in different parts of the world.

As if in defiance of Silicon Valley's hyperhumanist hopes for the emergence of Man 2.0, Bifo's ghostly nonheroes experience the psychosis of living in the hyperreal. In hyperreality, the mass shootings-cum-suicides on campuses and other gathering sites for youth from the United States to Norway mimic the recurrent aesthetic of the video game, where the terrorist attacks have already been seen before as doomsday-style media entertainment.[13] In the light of irresolvable distress, as well as corporeal and mental precarity, perhaps suicide does indeed become a way of enacting the "end of man" while hanging on to the remnants of self-sovereignty and dignity. This form of escape does not seem any more psychotic than the tech billionaires' dreams of escape to another planet.[14]

12. Berardi, *Heroes*, 145–6.

13. See Berardi, *Heroes*, 24.

14. This is precisely the argument outlined by Mark Fisher, a critic of capitalism who also wrote extensively about depression, in his uncannily prescient *Capitalist Realism: Is There No Alternative?* (Winchester, UK: Zero Books, 2009). Fisher took his own life in early 2017.

Intriguingly but also worryingly, those escapist dreams have recently taken a new form: time travel without relocation or expense. I am referring to the latest conceptual offering from our Silicon Valley saviors in the shape of the "simulation hypothesis": a *Matrix*-like belief that "what we experience as reality is actually a giant computer simulation created by a more sophisticated intelligence."[15] Embraced by, among others, Elon Musk of the abovementioned SpaceX and venture capitalist Sam Altman, a chairman of the OpenAI project, the simulation theory was laid down by philosopher Nick Bostrom. Bostrom's 2003 paper on the topic opens with the following credo: "At least one of the following propositions is true: (1) the human species is very likely to go extinct before reaching a 'posthuman' stage; (2) any posthuman civilization is extremely unlikely to run a significant number of simulations of their evolutionary history (or variations thereof); (3) we are almost certainly living in a computer simulation."[16] Bostrom does not definitively state that the simulation thesis trumps the other two but considers it entirely plausible, with future technologically advanced civilizations running "detailed simulations of their forebears."[17] Based on the assumption of "substrate-independence"—a conviction that life is just a set of computational processes that can be enacted in any medium[18]—this form of disembodied posthumanism, famously taken to task by N. Katherine Hayles in *How*

15. Olivia Solon, "Is Our World a Simulation? Why Some Scientists Say It's More Likely than Not," *Guardian,* October 11, 2016, https://www.theguardian.com/technology/2016/oct/11/simulated-world-elon-musk-the-matrix.

16. Nick Bostrom, "Are You Living In a Computer Simulation?," *Philosophical Quarterly* 53, no. 211 (2003): 243–55, http://www.simulation-argument.com/simulation.html.

17. Bostrom, "Computer Simulation?"

18. Bostrom, "Computer Simulation?"

We Became Posthuman, differs from what has become known as the "critical posthumanism" making waves in cultural theory over the last decade or so.[19] In a similar vein to my future-looking political concept of "the end of man," critical posthumanism sees the posthuman as an opening toward a different conceptualization of subjectivity beyond the limitations of the singular, liberal, human subject, with its gender-, race-, and powerblindness.

Unlike the posthumanism (or transhumanism) of Bostrom, the current AI brigade, and the cyberneticists of yesteryear, critical posthumanism embraces complexity, distribution, and context dependency as necessary for the conceptualization of life. While it recognizes that various kinds of high-level computational processes can occur in different media, and that future experiments with simulation and consciousness may no doubt surprise or even supersede our present selves, it also adopts a "situated"[20] notion of life as a process to be seen across a whole organism or even clusters of organisms.[21] Everything else be-

19. Radically critical thinking about the idea of the human can be traced back at least to the work of Charles Darwin and Sigmund Freud, and can also be found in the subsequent writings of such authors as Michel Foucault, Jacques Derrida, and Donna Haraway. Some of the more recent key texts that have critically engaged with the concept of posthumanism include: N. Katherine Hayles, *How We Became Posthuman: Virtual Bodies in Cybernetics, Literature, and Informatics* (Chicago: University of Chicago Press, 1999); Cary Wolfe, *What Is Posthumanism?* (Minneapolis: University of Minnesota Press, 2009); Rosi Braidotti, *The Posthuman* (Cambridge, UK: Polity Press, 2013); and Stefan Herbrechter, *Posthumanism: A Critical Analysis* (London: Bloomsbury, 2013).

20. See Donna Haraway, "Situated Knowledges: The Science Question in Feminism and the Privilege of Partial Perspective," *Feminist Studies* 14, no. 3 (Autumn 1998): 575–99.

21. See Lynn Margulis and Dorian Sagan, *What Is Life?* (Berkeley: University of California Press, 2000).

comes a metaphysical game in which this nebulous substance called life, like the ancient *nous* or the Christian soul, can be transferred to higher-level computation systems beyond any material forms that constitute it. This is not to say that critical posthumanism cannot imagine a different embodiment of life beyond its current carbon dependency. It is rather to contest the possibility of introducing a radical structural caesura between the substrate (say, the carbon-based body) and the content (that is, this unchangeable life "thing" that can be unproblematically extricated from its substrate and transferred to another).

While Bifo remains alert to the damaging effects of living in the semiocapitalist simulation, the tech billionaires and other advocates of human enhancement and planetary or AI transcendence consider simulation just the next logical step in the development of technology on our planet. In fact, it may have already happened, with evidence supposedly provided by the fact that the universe "behaves mathematically and is broken up into pieces (subatomic particles) like a pixelated video game."[22] What Bostrom identifies as a *"naturalistic theogony"* of his simulated world is therefore just a version of the current politico-economic system, with structuralist computer-game aesthetics used to explain supposedly eternal natural laws.[23] As Bostrom imagines it:

> In some ways, the posthumans running a simulation are like gods in relation to the people inhabiting the simulation: the posthumans created the world we see; they are of superior intelligence; they are "omnipotent" in the sense that they can interfere in the workings of our world even in ways that violate its physical laws; and they are "omniscient" in the sense that they can monitor ev-

22. Olivia Solon, "Is Our World a Simulation?"
23. Bostrom, "Computer Simulation?" (emphasis in original)."

erything that happens. However, all the demigods except those at the fundamental level of reality are subject to sanctions by the more powerful gods living at lower levels.[24]

There is something reassuring about the metaphysical fantasy of the simulation theory because it promises the rich and powerful that things will change while also staying the same, at least for those in charge. This story is thus music to the ears of the current theocracy of Silicon Valley billionaires, who are increasingly in the business of accompanying or even replacing states when it comes to the delivery of our basic services and the governance of our lives. It is because they see themselves as already having transcended toward the status of *Homo deus,* with their capital offering the promise of a bodily upgrade, immortality (typically described as "solving the death problem"), or a planetary exit. Others, less capable and less successful, will have to slot neatly into this new naturalized cyberscape.

It is interesting that Silicon Valley has been relatively quiet on the Anthropocene and climate-change front, preferring to rebrand all kinds of planetary issues as technological problems that require technological fixes. The apocalypticism of the Anthropocene narrative does not sit well with the teleological optimism of the tech billionaires, yet the latter mood is arguably the offshoot of the former. The Anthropocene narrative is a kind of "great leveller" not because it treats all humans as equally "guilty" of despoiling the Earth but rather because it carries with it a form of finalist political schadenfreude.[25] In the extinction event, the rich will finally be equal with the poor

---

24. Bostrom, "Computer Simulation?"
25. Etienne Turpin, "Who Does the Earth Think It Is, Now?," in *Architecture in the Anthropocene,* ed. Etienne Turpin (Ann Arbor, Mich.: Open Humanities Press, 2013), 3–10, 3. See also Joanna Zylinska, "Photography After the Human," *Photographies* 9, no. 2 (2016): 167–86.

and will go down all the same. In turn, Silicon Valley transcen-
dentalism, ostensibly engaged in combating global problems in
order to "make the world a better place," in fact avoids any radical planetary transformation while leaving the escape hatch
open for the "god class."

A Feminist Counterapocalypse

IN RESPONSE TO THE APOCALYPTIC TENOR of the dominant discourses of the Anthropocene, I want to outline an alternative microvision: the prospect of a feminist counterapocalypse that takes seriously the geopolitical unfoldings on our planet while also rethinking our relations *to* and *with* it precisely *as relations*. Relationality, I suggest, offers a more compelling model of subjectivity. Instead of positing a human subject that is separate from the world he (*sic*) inhabits and in which he can make interventions, it acknowledges *the prior existence of relations* between clusters of matter and energy that temporarily stabilize for us humans into entities—on a molecular, cellular, and social level. The relational model of subjectivity, involving a critical transfer of scientific ideas into a cultural context by feminist scholars such as Donna Haraway and Karen Barad, challenges the de facto masculinist subject that disinterestedly looks at the world as his possession and playground.[1] Recognizing that

1. See Donna Haraway, *The Companion Species Manifesto: Dogs, People, and Significant Otherness* (Chicago: Prickly Paradigm Press, 2003) and Karen Barad, *Meeting the Universe Halfway: Quantum Physics and the Entanglement of Matter and Meaning* (Durham, N.C.: Duke University Press, 2007).

we are *of* the world, it also presents instances of differentiation between subjects and objects as ethico-political tasks for the human. These tasks involve having to account for asymmetries of relations, making "agential cuts" to the arrangements of the world, and trying to establish better—that is, fairer and more just—relations.[2]

The concept of a feminist counterapocalypse builds Catherine Keller's idea: "A 'counter-apocalypse' recognizes itself as a kind of apocalypticism; but then it will try to interrupt the habit. . . . If counter-apocalypse reveals anything, it does so in ironic mimesis of the portentous tones of the original—with which it dances as it wrestles."[3] The microvision I am presenting here reflects and diffracts from the work of many other feminist thinkers who have attempted to cut the anthropos of the Anthropocene down to size not just by engaging in an explicit critique of gender relations in science and culture but also, more important, by challenging human exceptionalism, with its foundational subject, as a key framework for understanding the world. One such author with whom I would like to begin my feminist counterwalk through Anthropocene territory is Anna Lowenhaupt Tsing, whose book, *The Mushroom at the End of the World,* I briefly referred to earlier. "Following a mushroom," Tsing retraces the material and economic structurings of our "civilization" by drawing our attention to the relational ecologies developed from and around the fungi species called matsutake, both in the forest and on the market.[4] A delicacy in Japan, matsutake is relatively rare and needs to be sourced from places as remote as Oregon in the United States and Yunnan in China, thus establishing an intriguing global

2. Barad, *Meeting the Universe Halfway,* 140.
3. Keller, *Apocalypse Now and Then,* 19.
4. Tsing, *Mushroom,* viii.

network of growth, labor, and exchange. This socioeconomic network is woven into the already existent micronetwork of fungi ecologies that bind "roots and mineral soils, long before producing mushrooms."[5]

Tsing's book is set against the horizon of what we might term, with a nod to Haraway, a naturecultural ruin: the aftermath of climate change coupled with the collapse of the dream of industrial progress. Yet, rather than just lament the passing of the world as we (or at least some of us) know it, she sets off in search of "life in capitalist ruins." The socioeconomic context of her exploratory pursuit is provided by the situation of mastutake pickers in the forests of Oregon: a mixture of Southeast and East Asian immigrants from Cambodia, Laos, and China, as well as white Americans who have opted out, willingly or by turn of fate, of "what liberals think of as 'standard employment.'"[6] Reflecting on the precarious lives of the pickers, Tsing also lends an ear to the precarity of the ecologies, of various scales, in which they operate. Significantly, she then extends this idea of precarity, understood as "life without the promise of stability," from the situation affecting those placed outside privileged, or at least stable, socioeconomic circumstances to the structuring conditions of life in postindustrial capitalist economies.[7] In a similar tone to Bifo's argument about the radically destabilized nature of employment in the era of semiocapitalism, she recognizes that "now many of us, north and south, confront the condition of trouble without end."[8] For Tsing, precarity encompasses not only such phenomena as the increasing insecurity of the labor market but also environmen-

5. Tsing, *Mushroom*, viii.
6. Tsing, *Mushroom*, 77.
7. Tsing, *Mushroom*, 2.
8. Tsing, *Mushroom*, 2.

THE END OF MAN

tal threats on the level of individual species, as well as whole regions or even ecosystems, threatened with extinction. In what may seem like a surprising move, she then challenges the traditional view of precarity as "an exception to how the world works" and proposes we instead accept precarity as "the condition of our time."[9] This suggestion must not be mistaken for a sign of political resignation or withdrawal on Tsing's part, a peaceful embracing of our life among postindustrial ruins driven by a naïve desire to reconnect with our nonhuman others: forests, fungi, microbes. It is instead a deeply ethical proposal that redrafts the standalone subject of ethics as always already multiple, strange, and strange-to-itself. Such a subject does not have to open itself to others because it is already invaded, or contaminated, by them. However, it does have to undertake the effort of grasping this relationship as potentially mutually constitutive and therefore entailing a call to responsibility for others. Tsing writes:

> Precarity is the condition of being vulnerable to others. Unpredictable encounters transform us; we are not in control, even of ourselves. Unable to rely on a stable structure of community, we are thrown into shifting assemblages, which remake us as well as our others. We can't rely on the status quo; everything is in flux, including our ability to survive. Thinking through precarity changes social analysis. A precarious world is a world without teleology. Indeterminacy, the unplanned nature of time, is frightening, but thinking through precarity makes it evident that indeterminacy also makes life possible. The only reason all this sounds odd is that most of us were raised on dreams of modernization and progress.[10]

This responsibility for others and the willingness to be vulnerable to them should not of course be reduced to just being "nice"

---

9. Tsing, *Mushroom*, 20.
10. Tsing, *Mushroom*, 20.

to other people, or pets, or accepting any encounter or intrusion passively, be it with fungi or cancer cells. Rather, it entails the necessary task of recognizing that entanglement with others is not just a matter of our acceptance or good will, because it precedes the emergence of the human sense of the self.

Tsing's proposal can therefore be read as a radicalization of Judith Butler's ethics of precarity, developed from the work of Emmanuel Levinas. For Butler, ethics derives from the apprehension of the precariousness of the life of the Other: war victim, refugee, but also media-proclaimed enemy of the state, who is somewhat harder to empathize with.[11] This precariousness is manifested in the face or, more broadly, the figure of a vulnerable human who both threatens my sense of security and places a demand on me. The Other's demand is a form of accusation because it requires a justification of my relative comfort and stability when that Other is facing a political or even existential threat.[12] It thus introduces precarity as a shared condition of being human while also highlighting the fact that under particular sociopolitical circumstances, different humans experience precarity in different ways. The denial of precarity leads to the drawing of various lines of differentiation such as gender, race, class, or bodily ability. Levinas's ethics, and Butler's reworking of it, is no doubt humanist in that it adopts the human figure and voice as articulators of an ethical demand. Yet it also lends itself to a posthumanist opening because it poses a radical challenge to the self-sufficient and self-centered subject of moral theory.[13] In the ethics of responsibility toward the alterity of

11. Judith Butler, *Precarious Life: The Powers of Mourning and Violence* (London: Verso, 2004), xvii–xviii.

12. See Emmanuel Levinas, "Ethics As First Philosophy," in *The Levinas Reader,* ed. Sean Hand (Oxford: Blackwell, 1989).

13. See Joanna Zylinska, *Bioethics in the Age of New Media*

the Other, the moral subject is always already exposed, invaded, or, to use Tsing's phrase, contaminated. "Self-contained individuals," argues Tsing, are in turn "not transformed by encounter. Maximizing their interests, they use encounters—but remain unchanged in them."[14]

Tsing's implicit proposal for a nonnormative ethics of encounter—in which we are not told what to do but are faced with a call to responsibility—finds its most direct articulation in the invitation she issues to humans to embrace cross-species coexistence as an ethical way of being in the world. Learning the lesson of "collaborative survival" in precarious times from the matsutake mushroom, she argues that "staying alive—for every species—requires livable collaborations. Collaboration means working across difference, which leads to contamination. Without collaborations, we all die."[15] What is at stake in this model of understanding human–nonhuman relations is not the development of a flat yet ultimately banal ontology in which everything is connected with everything else, or the decision, as some may derisorily claim, of whether "I" am more (or less) important than a mushroom. Instead, what is really at stake here is the possibility of cutting down to size the supposedly unique human "I" by showing that this "I" is already, literally, made up of others.[16] But this possibility must also involve those capable of adopting the human "I" pronoun as theirs being able to recognize their ability to develop conscious ethical responses to this situation of ongoing material and ethical entanglement, beyond mere instinctive reactions to stimuli, and then being

(Cambridge, Mass.: MIT Press, 2009), 1–63.
   14. Tsing, *Mushroom*, 28.
   15. Tsing, *Mushroom*, 28.
   16. I am grateful to Piotr Boćkowski for infecting me with fungal thinking.

able to consolidate those responses into an ethical framework. Indeed, there is no way to unthink ourselves out of our human standpoint, no matter how much kinship or entanglement with "others" we identify. It is also next to impossible to abandon our human mode of perception and suspend the material and epistemological subject–object divisions we humans introduce into the flow of matter (including our primary positing of what surrounds us and makes us as "matter")—notwithstanding the misguided even if well-intentioned attempts to think like a bat, walk like a sheep, or float like a jellyfish. Rather than fantasize about some kind of ontological "species switch," the ethical task for us humans is not only to see ourselves as contaminated but also to account for the incisions we make in the ecologies of life, the differentiations and cuts we introduce and sustain, and the values we give to the entities we have carved out of these ecologies with our perceptual and cognitive apparatus.

A feminist counterapocalypse therefore unfolds from accepting the material condition of precarity without submitting to the "portentous tones" of the precarity discourse. In parodying apocalypse as the Armageddon for the White Man, it also embraces the "intensity" and the "drive for justice" entailed by its affective setup. The feminist counterapocalyptic framework creates a space for an ethical opening onto the precarious lives and bodies of human and nonhuman others—including the male bodies and minds that have been discarded in the downsizing process of disruptive semiocapitalism. In doing so, it promises liberation from the form of subjectivity pinned to a competitive, overachieving, and overreaching masculinity. It also prompts us all to ask: If unbridled progress is no longer an option, what kinds of coexistences and collaborations do we want to create in its aftermath?

Isabelle Stengers's concept of Gaia could perhaps serve as a model for, or figuration of, this mode of being (in) the world.

Gaia is derived from interdisciplinary Earth systems thinking, which adopts the dynamic interaction between the Earth's spheres—such as the atmosphere, hydrosphere, geosphere, and biosphere—as its unit of analysis. Not to be mistaken for a peaceful coexistence of entities under the banner of an un-reconstructed and benign "Nature," Gaia, at least in Stengers's use of this term, merely entails an attempt to shift the human observation point from the center of the action to its margins while simultaneously reducing in scale, scope, and significance the outcomes of human activity—without relieving humans of responsibility for the activities they do enact or participate in. Indeed, there is something rather demanding or even violent about Gaia, whose mode of appearance is that of "intrusion," because it reminds us that the Earth, in all its "systems," is not arranged for our pleasure or benefit.[17] In this sense, the notion of Gaia could be seen an alternative to the masculinist Anthropocene fantasy that ends up aggrandizing Man in the process. For Stengers, Gaia

> makes the epic versions of human history, in which Man, standing up on his hind legs and learning to decipher the laws of nature, understands that he is the master of his own fate, free from any transcendence, look rather old. Gaia is the name of an unprecedented or forgotten form of transcendence: a transcendence deprived of the noble qualities that would allow it to be invoked as an arbiter, guarantor, or resource; a ticklish assemblage of forces that are indifferent to our reasons and our projects.[18]

The adoption of this form of philosophical humility is only the first step, though. It needs to be followed up, according to

---

17. Isabelle Stengers, *In Catastrophic Times: Resisting the Coming Barbarism*, trans. Andrew Goffey (London: Open Humanities Press; Lüneburg, Germany: meson press, 2015), 58.
18. Stengers, *In Catastrophic Times*, 47.

Stengers, Tsing, and other counterapocalyptic thinkers of the end of the world, by embracing precarity as a political horizon against which the dream of infinite linear progress is presented as expired. For this horizon to be political rather than just aesthetically mournful, it needs to be inscribed with the aforementioned "drive for justice," which is not merely eschatological or pointed toward a celestial future. A political response arising out of this horizon may entail, after Stengers, working toward "the possibility of a future that is not barbaric" here on Earth while also giving up on a fantasy of peaceful coexistence between individuals, species, or systems.[19] Indeed, Tsing reminds us that opening the political horizon "to other beings shifts everything. Once we include pests and diseases, we can't hope for harmony; the lion will not lie down with the lamb. . . . The best we can do is to aim for 'good-enough' worlds, where 'good-enough' is always imperfect and under revision."[20] A feminist counterapocalypse that reworks finalism as a structuring condition of being in the world, while also issuing a responsibility for our entanglements with and in it, presents itself as both a less tragic and a less comical response to the Anthropocene narrative.

19. Stengers, *In Catastrophic Times*, 25.
20. Tsing, *Mushroom*, 255.

Coda: Sensing the Anthropocene

ALTHOUGH THIS BOOK uses a scholarly essay as its medium, it has been my ambition for a while now to try to outline a theoretical argument with media other than just words. In this case my photo film *Exit Man* offers an extension to my counterapocalyptic narrative. *Exit Man* uses my own photographs drawn from a kind of "local museum of the Anthropocene" I have been building for several years and supplements them with some archival images. It also features a voiceover reworked from the key threads of this book. The reasons for attempting this distributed mode of thinking that spills beyond the covers of the book or its digital file's lines of code are multifold. Nicholas Mirzoeff has argued that the Anthropocene, stretching back at least 250 years to the early days of fossil-fuel excavation and burning, cannot be *seen,* and hence *known,* by us contemporary humans because of the vastness of time across which it occurs. "It can only be visualized," singularly yet repeatedly.[1] Such visualizations take the form of not only poetic mistiness in paintings such as Claude Monet's 1873 *Impression: Sun Rising,* which Mirzoeff interprets in terms of coal smog, but also of postin-

1. Nicholas Mirzoeff, "Visualizing the Anthropocene," *Public Culture* 26, no. 2 (2014): 213–32, 213.

dustrial vistas showing depopulated landscapes in large-format art photographs by Andreas Gursky and Edward Burtynsky. Yet these visualizations embody and thus perpetuate the very same apocalyptic representational tropes. They show us what their authors want us to see and what we are capable of seeing, while also arguably obfuscating the most dramatic message of the Anthropocene narrative: the horror vacui, or the end of man and of everything else. In other words, they hide the fact that soon *there will be nothing to see*—and no one to see it. Thus, Anthropocene visuality ultimately has a pacifying effect. This is why we should first of all try to *unsee* the Anthropocene, suggests Mirzoeff, before we embark on anything else.

Arguably the Anthropocene presents us with a visual experience because it manifests itself to us humans through pollution-altered air, and hence light, and through the particulate matter that is reflected in this light. Yet the Anthropocence is not to be sensed only, or even primarily, on a visual level: we literally breathe it, day in, day out. The Anthropocene can therefore also be tasted, smelled, walked through, touched, and heard—as manifested in projects such as Tomás Saraceno's *Museo Aero Solar* made from plastic bags melted into giant floating sculptures that require "a sensitivity to the elements, especially as they are influenced by the sun," or DJ Spooky's "acoustic portrait" of the melting ice at the bottom of our globe, *Terra Nova: Sinfonia Antarctica*.[2] We could thus go so far as to say that we already sense the Anthropocene before we can come to terms with it; this is the case even if we ignore or deny it.

---

2. Tomás Saraceno, Sasha Engelmann, and Bronislaw Szerszynski, "Becoming Aerosolar: From Solar Sculptures to Cloud Cities," in *Art in the Anthropocene: Encounters among Aesthetics, Politics, Environments and Epistemologies*, eds. Heather Davis and Etienne Turpin (London: Open Humanities Press, 2015), 57–62, 61.

Exploring some *better* ways of sensing the Anthropocene is precisely how many artists have responded to the concept.[3] Going beyond the primary unconscious response of the body exposed to the elements, such artists have worked with ways of transforming our experience of the Anthropocene to produce a more engaging and more meaningful encounter beyond the "shock and awe" effect of the postindustrial sublime. Fabien Giraud and Ida Soulard have suggested that the incursion of the Anthropocene into the artistic domain has resulted in "the re-evaluation of art's relation to rationality."[4] For them, the force of the Anthropocene's geological temporality, which can be grasped but not seen, sutures the established epistemological partitions so that "any clear distinction between what we can *feel* of the world's movements and what we can *know* of them—any characteristically modern divides between the sensible and the intelligible—come to be fused and erased."[5] Significantly, Giraud and Soulard do not advocate relegating our encounters with issues of climate change and planetary transformation to an art "panic room" where we can only experience, and perhaps even take delight in, the horror of the planetary apocalypse. Instead they claim that "positioning ourselves within this turbulent landscape requires a taking hold, again, of epistemological questions."[6] We have here an intriguing proposal for an embedded and embodied experience of the Anthropocene,

---

3. My PhD student Sasha Litvintseva's theory-practice project of "geological filmmaking" is another example of trying to sense the Anthropocene via different media.

4. Fabien Giraud and Ida Soulard, "The Marfa Stratum: Contribution to a Theory of Sites," in *Art in the Anthropocene*, eds. Heather Davis and Etienne Turpin (London: Open Humanities Press, 2015), 167–80, 167.

5. Giraud and Soulard, "The Marfa Stratum," 167.

6. Giraud and Soulard, "The Marfa Stratum," 168.

one coupled with the need to *reflect on that experience* and on the very structuring of the concepts through which it is presented to us. Even though, as argued earlier, the Anthropocene envelops all our senses, its presentations, often unfolding as part of the climate-change visualization agenda, are frequently picture based. The typical visual tropes of climate change and environmental disaster through which we are made to see the Anthropocene involve "a polar bear on a piece of melting ice, . . . an aerial image of an oil spill, . . . a factory spewing filth into the sky."[7]

Picking up the above injunction to *see and sense better,* I want to cast *The End of Man* as an invitation, issued to those embodied humans who still recognize themselves as such, to look around, take a deep breath, and set out to carve a new path between the familiar and the possible. The image-ideas gathered in this book, and also those that spill beyond it, are intended as stepping stones that can hopefully lead us toward traversing not just the *human* imperialism of the colonial era that Mirzoeff rightly appends to the Anthropocene but also the *humanist* imperialism of the Anthropocene era.[8] In the latter, Man has succeeded in elevating himself above the complex planetary processes to (re)claim a godlike position: that of the maker and destroyer of worlds. Yet, as Cohen and Colebrook poignantly highlight: "The formation of a 'we' is generated from destruction and from the recognition of destruction: humanity as global anthropos comes into being *with* the Anthropocene, with the declaration that there is a unity to the species, and that this unity lies in its power to mark the planet."[9] Chipping away at

7. Trevor Paglen, *The Last Pictures* (Berkeley: University of California Press, 2012), 13.

8. See Mirzoeff, "Visualizing the Anthropocene," 217.

9. Cohen and Colebrook, preface to *Twilight,* 8.

the apocalyptic habit that is also the foundation of man's always fictitious unity, *The End of Man,* together with its photofilmic component, *Exit Man,* aims to help us rethink and resense both the Anthropocene and ourselves as humans *in* and *with* the Anthropocene. It also hopes to make us see ourselves on the ground and hear a different—less stern, even if not less serious—story of our planet and its various species.

Watch the *Exit Man* film by scanning the QR code below or visiting this link: https://vimeo.com/203887003.

Acknowledgments

Warm thanks to Gary Hall, Nina Sellars, and Stelarc for their comments on earlier versions of the book and the film. The penultimate section of the book, "A Feminist Counterapocalypse," was originally written as a catalog essay for the exhibition "The World to Come" at the University of Florida Gainesville (2018). I am grateful to curator Kerry Oliver-Smith for the invitation and inspiration.

Joanna Zylinska is professor of new media and communications at Goldsmiths, University of London, a photomedia artist, and author of six books, including *Nonhuman Photography* and *Minimal Ethics for the Anthropocene*.

CPSIA information can be obtained
at www.ICGtesting.com
Printed in the USA
FFOW03n1445190418
46307359-47855FF

9 781517 905590